The Cen

A SHORT HISTORY

by

M. A. C. Horne

1987
Published by Douglas Rose
35 Summers Lane, North Finchley, London N12 0PE
but
Distributed by Nebulous Books
12 Raven Square, Alton, Hampshire GU34 2LL

THE CENTRAL LINE

HISTORICAL MAP

Some of the stations on the Central Line have been renamed since opening; the names shown here are present ones. Readers requiring fuller details are referred to *The London Underground: A Diagrammatic History* also published by Douglas Rose; this colour diagram shows opening and closing dates and all station name changes for the whole Underground system.

EASTERN COUNTIES AND GREAT EASTERN RAILWAYS TO ONGAR AND NEWBURY PARK

The service between Leyton and Loughton was opened by the Eastern Counties Railway on 22nd August 1856 and constituted most of a new branch line which began at Stratford. The ECR became part of the Great Eastern Railway system in 1862 and the Loughton branch was extended to Ongar on 24th April 1865, the station at Loughton being moved from its initial location to a point on the extension line at the same time. On 1st May 1903 a GER loop line opened to passengers from a junction north of Woodford to Newbury Park, thence onwards to Ilford. The GER became part of the LNER system in 1923, and British Railways (Eastern Region) in 1948, and London Transport Underground trains were projected on the dates shown here, the connections with the main line railway being severed later.

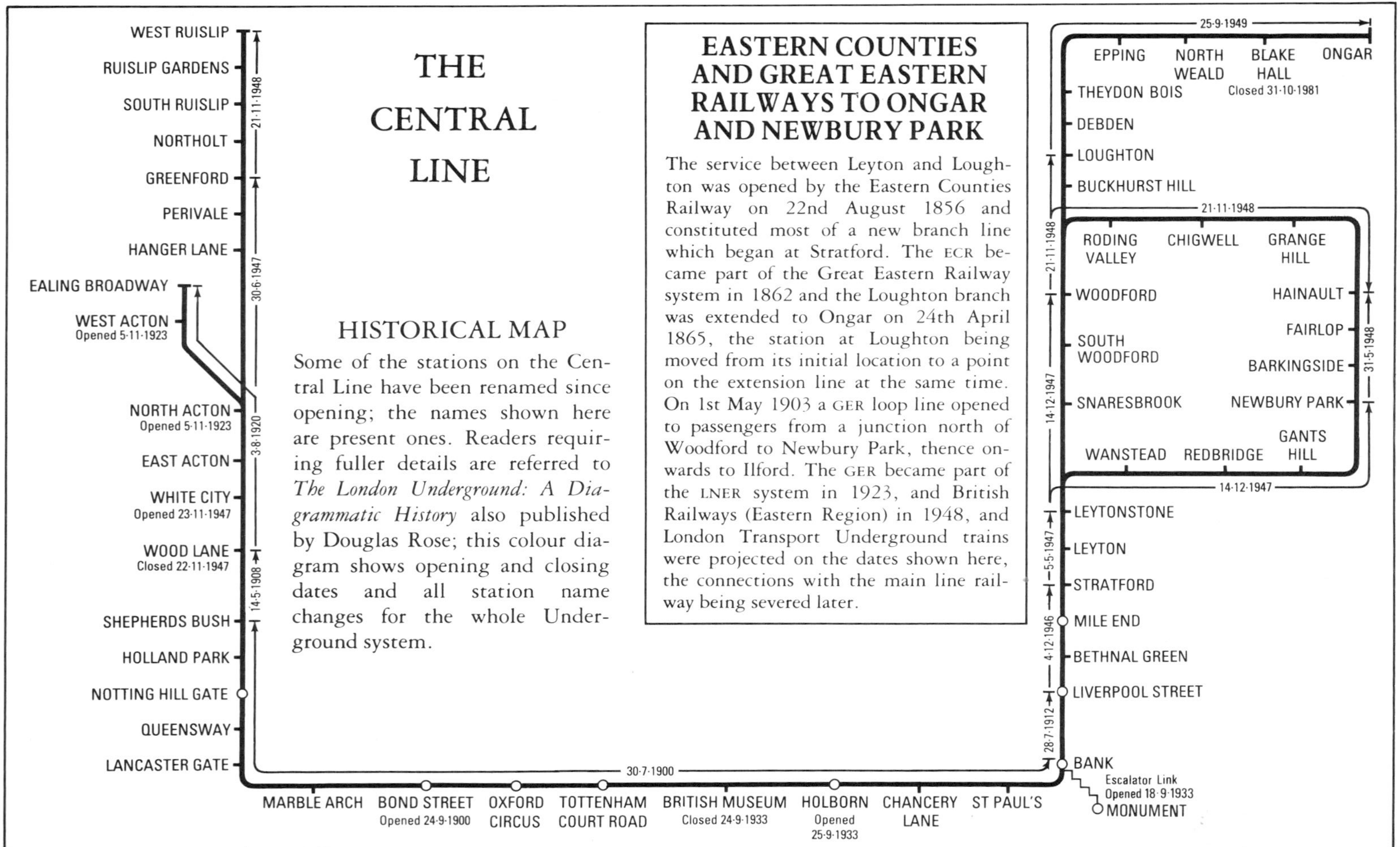

WEST RUISLIP
RUISLIP GARDENS
SOUTH RUISLIP
NORTHOLT
GREENFORD
PERIVALE
HANGER LANE
EALING BROADWAY
WEST ACTON
Opened 5·11·1923
NORTH ACTON
Opened 5·11·1923
EAST ACTON
WHITE CITY
Opened 23·11·1947
WOOD LANE
Closed 22·11·1947
SHEPHERDS BUSH
HOLLAND PARK
NOTTING HILL GATE
QUEENSWAY
LANCASTER GATE
21·11·1948
30·6·1947
3·8·1920
14·5·1908
30·7·1900
MARBLE ARCH
BOND STREET
Opened 24·9·1900
OXFORD CIRCUS
TOTTENHAM COURT ROAD
BRITISH MUSEUM
Closed 24·9·1933
HOLBORN
Opened 25·9·1933
CHANCERY LANE
ST PAUL'S
BANK
Escalator Link
Opened 18·9·1933
MONUMENT
28·7·1912
LIVERPOOL STREET
BETHNAL GREEN
4·12·1946
MILE END
STRATFORD
5·5·1947
LEYTON
LEYTONSTONE
14·12·1947
WANSTEAD
REDBRIDGE
GANTS HILL
NEWBURY PARK
BARKINGSIDE
FAIRLOP
HAINAULT
31·5·1948
SNARESBROOK
SOUTH WOODFORD
WOODFORD
RODING VALLEY
CHIGWELL
GRANGE HILL
21·11·1948
BUCKHURST HILL
LOUGHTON
DEBDEN
THEYDON BOIS
EPPING
NORTH WEALD
BLAKE HALL
Closed 31·10·1981
ONGAR
25·9·1949

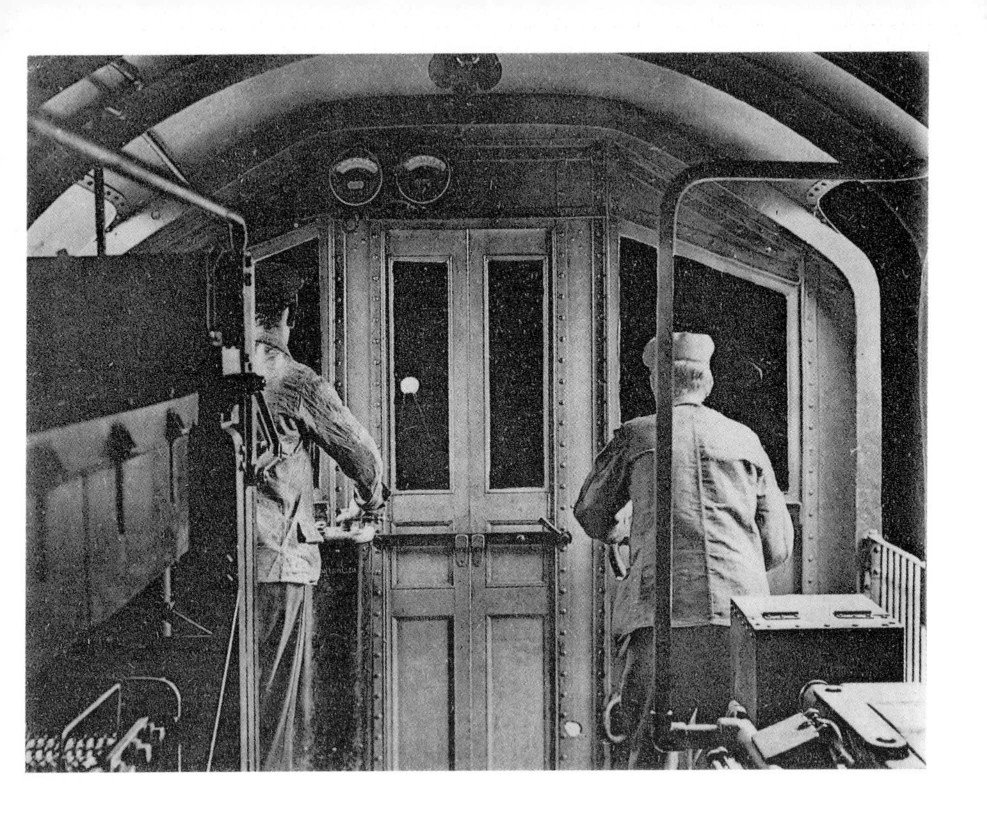

View towards the front of one of the 1903 Motor Cars taken from the switch compartment: the driver on the left and assistant on the right. *M.A.C.Horne collection*

To C. E. L.

The Central Line: A Short History
by M. A. C. Horne
ISBN 1 870354 01 X
First published in November 1987

Other short histories in this series by M. A. C. Horne
THE NORTHERN LINE

The author and publisher wish to acknowledge the assistance of
George Jasieniecki, John Liffen, Jonathan Roberts and Suzanne Tagg.

Photographs marked with an asterisk (*) are reproduced
by kind permission of the London Transport Museum.
Copy prints may be ordered from the Museum's Photo
Library.

The text in this book has been set in
Linotype Garamond No.3 10/11pt and 8/8½pt,
with appropriate italic and small caps,
and Bembo Bold, on a Linotron 202.

Typeset by Douglas Rose, London N12 0PE.
Cover design by Art Attack, London SW9 6AR,
from an idea by M. A. C. Horne.
Printed by Haynes Cannon, Wellingborough NN8 3QX.

THE CENTRAL LINE holds the distinction of providing the longest possible train journey on the Underground without a change, from Epping to West Ruislip, a journey of 34·1 miles (54·9km). With 51 stations spread along the 52 route miles of track it is also unusual in embracing one of the most heavily used sections of the Underground (Liverpool Street to Stratford) with the most lightly used (Epping to Ongar). In meandering into rural Essex the Central Line provides a service quite different from that which could have been imagined by the engineers and businessmen in the late nineteenth century when the plans for what was then the Central London Railway were initially formulated. Quite how such changes came about it is the intention of this book to explain.

The earliest underground railways in London, the Metropolitan and Metropolitan District, were steam-hauled concerns operating in cutting or double track tunnels just beneath street level. Between the two of them, what is now the Circle Line was constructed between 1863 and 1884. Parliament had been reluctant to allow the main line railways to encroach too closely into central London and the Circle Line was then looked upon as a means of linking many of the termini, both with each other and with the City. This left a considerable area without convenient railway access, notably the increasingly important West End districts. Street congestion was as much a problem then as it is now, if not somewhat worse, and in spite of the cabs for hire and extensive horse bus services (some operated by the railways), towards the close of the century there was a demand for railway services closer to the centre which was not being met.

The course of transport development in central London changed dramatically when the City & South London Railway (C&SLR) opened in 1890. Two factors made this railway very different from what had gone before. Firstly the method of construction, which utilized shield-driven, circular, iron-lined tunnels at a deep level through the London clay. This involved minimal disruption at street level as the low level works were serviced through a number of vertical shafts where there were small working sites. The second breakthrough was the use of electric traction for the first time in London. This was very much more flexible than steam traction as well as being cleaner and able to support a more intensive service. Steam traction would also have been impracticable for working deep level tubes.

The route from the City of London via Newgate Street, Oxford Street and the Bayswater Road was one of some antiquity and of long standing importance. Bisecting the Circle Line (which was far from circular) across its greater axis it became a natural object of attention from speculative railway promoters, and it was indeed a congested route which might benefit from relief by a railway. Schemes for railways between Marble Arch and the City are known as early as 1865 but failed either because of financial difficulties or because the promoters were unable to persuade Parliament to provide the necessary powers.

The Parliamentary success of the City & Southwark Subway (an earlier name for the City & South London Railway) in 1884, together with subsequent evidence that construction was proceeding successfully, not unnaturally created pressure for more such schemes. Several tube railways were promoted from 1886 although none were sanctioned by Parliament until the C&SLR had actually opened. Two of these proposals were for railways along the Oxford Street axis. The London Central Subway envisaged a railway from Shepherds Bush to a point just east of the Tottenham Court Road while the Central London Railway (CLR) anticipated a line from Bayswater (Queens Road) to the City.

Of these two schemes only the Central London came before Parliament in the 1889-90 session. The Bill provided for the railway to be authorized in three sections, in total running from the western terminus along the Bayswater Road, Oxford Street, High Holborn, Newgate Street, Cheapside and thence via King William Street to a junction with the City & South London Railway, a total of 4·67 miles (7·52km). After a considerable battle in the House of Commons the Bill was eventually approved but their Lordships were harder to persuade and after much debate it was rejected; during the parliamentary process the connection with the C&SLR was dropped and the proposed railway was cut back to a site in Cornhill.

The Central London directors refused to accept defeat and spent some time adjusting the Bill to meet the principal objections. One significant change was made to the proposed alignment in that the London Central Subway proposal was embraced by extending the western terminus to Shepherds Bush. A further battle ensued in the next session of Parliament when unconvinced MPs and Peers were slowly persuaded of the benefits to be reaped from the line. Amid a fourteenfold increase in the restrictive clauses, the Bill received the Royal Assent on 5th August 1891.

In 1892 the new company successfully applied to Parliament for authority to substitute a station outside the Royal Exchange for the authorized site for Bank station in Cornhill, and to extend the eastern terminus to Liverpool Street. This served to increase the ire of the Metropolitan Railway as the new tube would now directly short-circuit the north side of the Circle Line – it was already somewhat put out that the scheme had been authorized at all. In the event it had little immediate fear since it was some time before

Construction of Central London Railway running tunnels by means of the Thomson excavator. The bucket conveyor which attacked the working face and removed the clay is clearly shown. *J.Liffen collection*

the interloper could get its proposal under way — Parliament had to authorize an extension of time in 1894 for both the compulsory land acquisition and for completion of the works.

The company had anticipated that construction of the line would be sponsored by a mining finance organization called the Exploration Company Limited. With this in mind it offered its share prospectus to the public in June 1895. Although the public had not shown much interest in contemporary tube schemes the Railway had been hopeful: the technical success of the C&SLR had become apparent and with the benefit of the experience of that line, together with a much better route, the CLR ought to have been a promising enterprise. Nevertheless the public response was very disappointing and it was only when Sir Ernest Cassel, through the Exploration Company, was able to find the major part of the construction costs that the railway was saved.

The construction work was given to the Electric Traction Company, specifically created to act as main contractors. In turn the tunnelling work was subcontracted to three different firms which each built a section of the line, these contracts being let early in 1896; land acquisition had been started the previous year. Construction started in April 1896 at the Chancery Lane station site and by September the shaft there had been sunk and those at some other stations were well in progress; by the end of the year most shafts had been sunk and tunnelling was in full swing. Meanwhile the CLR had been negotiating with both the North London and Great Eastern Railways about their respective connections with the new tube station at Liverpool Street. Unfortunately, towards the end of 1896, the anticipated agreement with the Great Eastern Railway had failed to materialize and the CLR Board opted not to proceed with the extension, although they did decide to utilize their construction powers from Bank to a point about a third of the way along Old Broad Street in order to provide a pair of reversing sidings.

The majority of the tunnelling was performed using Greathead shields, where miners excavated the clay within the protection of a metal drum (the shield) which was periodically forced forward into the clay ahead by pneumatic rams. The exposed tunnel behind the shield was immediately lined with cast-iron segments which had an internal diameter of about 11ft 8ins (3·6m), and allowed for a concrete lining which brought the internal diameter down to 11ft 6ins (3·5m); in the event the concreting was considered an extravagance and only short sections of the tunnels near stations were actually lined. On curves a larger diameter of tunnel was used which allowed for the overhang of the carriages. The Central London was also a testing ground for some power-assisted tunnelling. Part of the line was built using a Thomson excavator. This was in effect an electrically-driven bucket conveyor where one end was pivoted such that the other could be swung to make contact with any point on the tunnel face. The ground ahead was gradually chewed away by teeth at the end of the quickly-moving buckets which also removed the spoil. A second device was the John Price rotary excavator. This was a shield with a rotating framework at the leading end upon which cutting teeth were mounted. The rotating end was forced against the tunnel face and the teeth cut away at the clay, removed by conveyor, allowing the shield to be moved forward. Although the rotary excavator was to have an important future it proved difficult to steer accurately in this pioneer application, especially on curves, and its use was therefore rather limited.

The stations were to be provided at Bank, Post Office, Chancery Lane, British Museum, Tottenham Court Road, Oxford Circus,

Bond Street, Marble Arch, Lancaster Gate, Queens Road, Notting Hill Gate, Holland Park and Shepherds Bush. All were to consist of a pair of separate iron-lined tunnels of 21ft 6ins (6·6m) diameter, and in each case access would be gained by lifts from surface level; generally, the lifts would carry passengers to a low level landing from where a short passage and stairway would take them to platform level. It should perhaps be noted that prior to opening certain stations were widely known by different names. Principally, Bond Street was to have been Davies Street, British Museum was to have been Bloomsbury and Lancaster Gate was to have been Westbourne.

At Bank a ticket hall was constructed beneath the road junction, and by agreement with the City Corporation an elliptical subway was to pass around the ticket hall and connect with various street corners by means of seven subway passages. A considerable number of gas, water and telegraph services existed beneath this busy intersection and these were redirected around the site through a pipe subway built beneath the public one. The work at this station proved exceptionally difficult. Although the work was started in 1895 it was not until early 1898 that the utility services could be diverted into the pipe subway which freed the site for sinking the first pair of lift shafts — the remainder were in progress by the end of the year. The works at Bank progressed more slowly than had been hoped and a further extension of time was needed from Parliament.

At Post Office (now St Paul's), Chancery Lane and Notting Hill Gate the platforms were not at the same level, which resulted from the need to keep the line of the railway beneath public streets to avoid paying compensation to the property owners above. At other stations the platforms were arranged next to each other and there were cross passages between them. The Bond Street station site presented a slight problem and it looked for a while that an alternative site would be needed — powers were even sought. In the end this did not prove necessary and the original site was used but construction was somewhat delayed. At Notting Hill Gate the CLR station was situated close to but discrete from that of the Metropolitan Railway, and there was no intention of providing any form of direct interchange between the two.

By the end of 1898 all the tunnelling had been completed except for 100 yards near Bank and during the following year most of the track laying took place and the erection of station buildings was started, though there were delays because of a shortage of steelwork. The lift installation work was also well in progress. Electrical equipment and the locomotives were also delivered during this time and in March 1900 the railway was sufficiently complete to

A contemporary commercial postcard showing the CLR station at Notting Hill Gate. The rear horse-drawn bus (to Liverpool Street) is of interest in illustrating the main form of competition. *M.A.C.Horne collection*

allow some trial running to take place.

The railway was ready for the formal opening on 27th June 1900 and the ceremony was performed by the Prince of Wales (soon to become King Edward VII) who some ten years previously had opened the pioneer tube, the City & South London Railway. The most striking difference between the two would have been the very much more generous proportions of the Central London compared with the C&SLR – larger trains and longer platforms, for example. Arriving at Bank he then travelled by train to the depot at Shepherds Bush where the formal opening ceremony took place. It was another month before the public was admitted, on 30th July, and in the intervening period a trial service of empty trains was operated.

Given the busy traffic corridor beneath which it ran, the new railway could scarcely fail to have been well patronized. Traffic levels quickly rose as the public tested the new railway – they liked it. Receipts during the first week were £4323 and seem to have been obtained largely at the expense of the bus companies (the receipts of the London General Omnibus Company and the London Road Car Company had, between them, dropped by £2732; the other underground lines being little affected). One feature which assisted its popularity was the flat fare of twopence. This echoed the system of charging on the C&SLR for the previous ten years (although it had just abandoned this in favour of distance related fares). Some elements of the press immediately dubbed the line the "Twopenny Tube" and the name caught on, at least for a while. Workman's tickets were also available at twopence return. (It should be recalled that prior to 1971 there were 240 pence to the pound and not 100, as now. In terms of spending power twopence, at the turn of the century, represents about 25 to 45 pence today).

Tickets were issued at the booking offices but were collected and cancelled prior to travel, although certain changes were soon made to avoid certain misuses which were discovered. From opening to the end of the year nearly £120,000 revenue was collected from nearly 15 million passengers, and this represented a profit of £39,000 – enough for the directors to declare a dividend of 2½ per cent. Initially a 5-minute service was operated, increased as necessary at busy times.

The depot was situated on a twenty acre site to the north of Shepherds Bush alongside Wood Lane, and access was gained by a single-track connection rising to the surface from the west end of Shepherds Bush station. Although steep, the link was well within the capability of the locomotives for hauling the trains and it was not the burden that the Stockwell depot access had proved to be to the City & South London. The depot comprised carriage and locomotive repair shops, a six-road engine shed and a twelve-road carriage shed 360 feet (109·7m) long. An unusual feature was a loop line which ran round the back of the sheds and allowed complete trains to be turned if necessary. There was also a connection with the West London Railway which, amongst other things, allowed for the easy delivery of coal to the power house.

The interior of the car shed at Wood Lane showing the gate-ends of the end carriages.
Electrical Review

The depot had not originally been constructed large enough to store all the carriages overnight and some outstabling in tunnel stations was contemplated, inspection pits being provided. This was soon seen as a serious error and a second twelve-road car shed was built on the site of paved carriage-cleaning sidings; this appears to have come into use in 1902 and three of the roads were soon equipped with pits. The station pits were apparently then covered over.

In the absence of any remotely suitable outside supply the railway had to construct its own generating plant. The power station was erected at the Wood Lane depot and was very powerful for the day, the plant and distribution system being novel in this country. Steam was raised by 16 Babcock & Wilcox coal-fired boilers, and the six generators were driven each by their own engines which were of the Reynolds-Corliss reciprocating type built by the American firm of Allis; each of these was designed to operate at 1250hp rating, but could uprated by about 60 per cent if required. At first, the service could be worked by any five of the generators being operated at once. The generators were supplied by the American General Electric Company (GEC) and produced three-phase alternating current at the (then high) pressure of 5000 volts. Each generator was rated at 850kW capacity. To allow for future expansion, provision was made for a further two generators (and four boilers) to be installed later.

From the power house high tension current was distributed to substations at Notting Hill Gate, Marble Arch and Post Office where the plant was installed in the base of the lift shafts. Each substation was equipped with transformers which stepped down the feeder voltage to 330 volts a.c., and this was fed to the track through rotary converters which produced an output of 550 volts d.c.. Like the C&SLR, current was supplied to the locomotives through a single conductor rail and returned through the running rails. The conductor rail was at a slightly higher level (1½ ins, or 38mm) than the running rails and was situated mid-way between them. The purchase and installation of the electrical equipment for the line, and the power house, was the responsibility of the British Thomson-Houston company (BTH). It was a matter of some regret to the British engineering industry that most of the equipment was in fact brought over from America; *The Engineer* claimed that this was because at the crucial time when contracts were being let there was an engineering strike in progress and British companies could not offer the necessary guarantees for delivery.

The electrical power supply system proved quite robust although it was the subject of some early modifications. Initially the high tension supply to all the substations ran through common feeder

One of the CLR locomotives shortly after delivery. The huge controller unit can be seen inside the cab. *M.A.C.Horne collection*

cables and an emergency lighting supply was available from storage batteries. Both these features were soon considered undesirable and it was decided to build an additional substation at Bond Street, with independent feeder cables. However, there had been a serious electrical fire at the Notting Hill Gate substation which suggested that lift shaft bases were not ideal locations for substations and several changes to the layout had been necessary at all three. It was now deemed prudent to build the new substation at Bond Street at surface level, even though it was primarily intended only as a standby facility for lift and lighting supplies (but could also substitute for a traction substation should the need arise). A further standby substation was later built at top level at Post Office. The Power House was considered very successful, although coal consumption was initially high and occasional black smoke created some acrimony with the local authority and the CLR was taken to court. Additional generating capacity was soon installed, together with a rotary converter which supplemented the existing substations.

The Central London Railway had originally intended to use a pair of electric locomotives, one at each end of the train, and with the locomotive at the rear controlled from the one at the front. This system would have been similar in principle to that used on the Waterloo & City Railway (opened in 1898) although in that case the motors had been mounted on the end carriages. However such

Side elevation of a Brush built carriage of 1900 vintage as delivered. The extra gate at the right-hand end would have been coupled to the next carriage along.

M.A.C.Horne collection

a system required a number of high-capacity wires running along the length of the train, in effect carrying traction current. The Board of Trade were rather unhappy about the fire risk this method of control presented in the confines of a tube tunnel, and had refused to sanction this type of operation on any tube railway built since the Waterloo & City. A single locomotive per train was therefore required on the CLR.

Twenty-eight electric locomotives were provided, being designed and built in America by GEC, then shipped to Britain in kit form and erected at Wood Lane. They were powerful machines with a body of the 'camel-back' type, with a central cab, mounted on twin bogies with each of the four axles powered by its own motor. The total weight was 43·93 tons (44·28 tonnes). A single controller was provided centrally within the cab and hand-notching the control handle was necessary, which included series-parallel switching. Duplicate instruments were provided to allow for the locomotives running in either direction. The Westinghouse air brake was provided and each locomotive carried its own air compressor. During service running each locomotive was manned by a driver and an assistant.

The trains were designed to be formed of a locomotive and up to seven coaches. During the first months of operation there totalled 150 coaches of which 125 were built by the Ashbury Railway Carriage & Iron Company and 25 by the Brush Electrical Engineering Company; a further 18 carriages were delivered by Ashbury's in 1901. Each carriage was 45ft 6ins (13·8m) long overall, of which the wooden body was 39 feet (11·6m) and the remainder was occupied by the gated end platforms. Not only were the carriages longer than those on the C&SLR but they were also of a somewhat larger cross-section as the ruling minimum tunnel diameter was 11ft 6ins (3·5m) as compared with 10ft 2ins (3·1m) on the older line. Each car contained 48 seats, some arranged longitudinally and some transversely, and straps were provided for standing passengers. Each train was manned by two guards (one at each end of the train) with gatemen at the intermediate gangways.

Interior of one of the original Brush carriages shortly before delivery in 1900. The upholstery in some of the later cars was not as plush as this. *M.A.C.Horne collection*

In addition to the electric locomotives the CLR also owned two steam locomotives, built by the Hunslet Engine Company in 1899. These surprising 0-6-0 side tank machines were built to the tube loading gauge and were originally purchased by the contractors to assist with construction work. The CLR soon found them invaluable for shunting in the yard. They could burn coal in the open air, but to make life easier in the tunnels they were equipped with oil-burning and steam condensing apparatus. Coupling and buffing gear was fitted to suit coupling both to main line wagons and CLR stock. In due course the tunnel work was at least partially undertaken by battery-operated cars and the steam locomotives spent much of their life in Wood Lane yard. One of the locomotives was dismantled and sold in 1920 and the other was disposed of the following year (but it may have been used on another line and a sighting in the yard at Lillie Bridge depot is reported as late as 1925). It should perhaps be mentioned here that most of Wood Lane depot initially contained unelectrified track and to enable some shunting to be performed by electric locomotive at least one of them was fitted with overhead trolley poles, and a system of overhead wiring was installed.

View along one of the new platforms at Queen's Road station (renamed Queensway in 1946) at about the time of the opening of the CLR. *Electrical Review*

The track laid in the tube sections was, at the time of opening, of 'bridge' cross section on longitudinal sleepers and subsequently gave some trouble, particularly at joints. All track laid in the tunnel was of 100 pounds per yard section although point and crossing work was executed in bull-head rail. Quite why this curious arrangement prevailed is perhaps explained by an incident recalled subsequently by a BTH engineer who remembered an incident a little while before the line opened: the BTH resident engineer burst into the office in great excitement to say that they had just been trying out the first locomotive and it was too large for the tunnel! It was claimed that the railway engineers had omitted to take into account the height of the rails, and the difficulty was partly overcome by fitting new springs to the locomotives and partly by laying shallow rails. The bridge rail was about 1½ inches (38mm) lower than equivalent bull-head rail.

At the low level, each station comprised two 325 feet (99m) long wooden platforms, with the station tunnels electrically lit and finished with brilliant white tiling. At street level, stations (other than Bank) consisted of neat single story buildings designed by

Harry Measures and finished in a light brown tiled surface described as unglazed terra-cotta. It appears that there were originally to have been upper stories to these buildings but towards the end of 1899 it was decided not to proceed with them for the time being.

Although stairs were provided at all the stations the usual means of communication between the upper and lower stations was by means of lifts. Hydraulic lifts had been customary in this country, but Frank Julian Sprague had developed electrically operated lifts successfully in America and was invited over in 1897 to present an electric lift scheme to the CLR. The company took quite some convincing, but the result was that on 14th June Sprague received a contract for the 48 lifts required. The shafts were already under construction and varied in size and quantity between the stations. In each case the equipment was installed in the bottom of the shafts and connected to the lift through a pulley at the top. The lift controller was inside the cars and the number of lifts per shaft was generally two or three, depending on shaft size; five shafts were provided at Bank, each containing one car per shaft.

The Shepherds Bush terminus soon proved to be exceedingly busy and the existing lifts were quite inadequate for the traffic. It was decided to enlarge the station and to install no less than four new lifts, two additional shafts being required. When tenders were received neither the price nor delivery times were regarded as acceptable for electric lifts and Messrs Waygood were therefore

Hunslet built steam locomotive constructed for the CLR contractors in 1899.

Real Photographs

invited to provide four electro-hydraulic lifts. These were brought into service towards the end of 1902 and made an interesting comparison with the existing Sprague lifts which were retained. In general the Sprague lifts had not initially proved over reliable and in the first six months breakdowns and periods out of service were common, but these early problems were largely eliminated.

Signalling was essentially of the traditional mechanical kind and was similar in principle to that used on the C&SLR, utilizing Sykes lock-and-block control. There were 16 signal cabins, one each at the ten stations where the platforms were at the same level and one on each platform at the three stations where they were at different levels. The starting signals were of the semaphore pattern but the home signals were simply a sliding spectacle. A brush on the rearmost bogie on each train made an electrical contact which released the section locking when the train had passed through.

Operationally the line was remarkably successful from the start, although there were a few derailments the causes of which were not immediately clear. One matter which did tax the management was the persistence of an unusual smell which manifested itself in the low level stations and tunnels. This proved quite innocuous although its source was not clear – nevertheless it was not considered to be a particularly desirable feature of the line and some effort was expended in dealing with it. Among the ideas considered was that of placing evergreen shrubs on the platforms. Like the C&SLR, no mechanical ventilation was originally considered necessary. Fans were, however, put in at the substations to keep the temperature down and an experiment was made at Post Office where this fan was used to draw out air from the platforms. This was considered a success and a large fan was soon installed at Bond Street where it was run for 3½ hours each night to pump stale air out of the tunnels. In 1903 another large fan was erected at the tunnel mouth at Wood Lane and a hinged door was used to seal the tunnel end. The company reported that the air was "considerably" improved. Various other fans were subsequently installed at stations along the line and later 'Ozonair' ventilation plants were introduced at a number of stations.

A rather more important difficulty facing the company was the objection by certain property owners along the route to the vibration being caused by the new railway. The Board of Trade (then responsible for supervising railway safety and operation) appointed a Committee of Inquiry to investigate. The Committee reported in February 1902, although the source of the problem had been identified long before then and was largely confined to the design of the locomotives. These machines had heavy traction motors where the armatures were mounted directly on the axles; most of

One of the original carriages converted into an experimental motor car with BTH control in 1901. Rather heavily retouched, the photograph is probably wanting in accuracy.
M.A.C.Horne collection

the locomotive weight was therefore unsprung and a considerable amount of vibration was transmitted to the track and tunnels. This design had been chosen mainly to avoid the use of gears which had been tried on other railways and had proved excessively noisy.

The CLR undertook several experiments to reduce the problem. Three locomotives were rebuilt to incorporate geared drives; this had the added benefit of enabling smaller, higher-speed motors to be used which reduced the total weight of the locomotives to 31 tons (31·5 tonnes) of which only about a third was unsprung. Another approach was the equipping of four coaches with motors and control equipment such that two six-coach trains were formed, both with the motored coaches at the outer ends. Each motor coach had one motor bogie with both axles equipped with their own motors (these were similar to those used on the geared locomotives, but smaller). The motor coaches weighed 23½ tons (24 tonnes) when laden. While the geared locomotives were a considerable improvement in terms of the transmitted vibration, the motor coach train was very much better still and the company looked to this method of operation as the solution to its problem.

Sixty-four new coaches were therefore ordered from British manufacturers: 24 from Brown Marshall (which became the Metropolitan Amalgamated Railway Carriage & Wagon Company) and 40 from the Birmingham Railway Carriage & Wagon Company; the bogies were built by BTH and Leeds Forge. Each vehicle was equipped with a driving cab at one end and these became known as Motor Cars (an American term) whilst the existing coaches became known as Trailer Cars, or Trailers. Each of the new motor cars was equipped with a system of control such that the operating gear for the motor equipment was operated through contactors fed from circuits which ran the length of the train. By this means heavy traction-load currents were not passed along the train but all the motors could nevertheless be operated from the controller (the 'master' controller) on the leading car — a system known as multiple unit control. This was a system invented by Sprague, in America, and was a development resulting from his work on electric lifts; the electrical equipment and traction motors were built by GEC in America.

It had been hoped to use an additional motor car in the middle of the train, as traffic demand required 7-car trains, but the Board of Trade was unhappy about the restriction this would impose on free passage along the train in an emergency and a trailer had to be used instead; more powerful motors were installed on the motor cars to compensate. Six additional trailers were also ordered from the Birmingham company (all-steel this time) to augment the fleet and two of the experimental motor cars were later converted back to trailers (the other two ended their days as part of the fleet reserved for engineering works). The new motor car trains began to enter service in April 1903 and the locomotives were finally superseded in June. Two of the locomotives were sold to the Metropolitan Railway towards the end of 1905 for experimental purposes, but it was not until 1906 before arrangements were made for disposing of material from a further 24 of them, which it appears were dismantled; two were retained.

The locomotive crew, whilst keeping a lookout in whichever direction they happened to be going, had always remained on one particular side of the machine and signal sighting was arranged accordingly. When the motor cars were delivered this practice was perpetuated, and all the cars facing in one direction had a right hand driving position while all those facing the other way had a left hand position (in later years the introduction of loop working which turned the trains around once per trip somewhat confused this system). The arrival of motor car trains also identified the need to equip some of the trailer cars with driving positions to enable a proportion of the 6-car trains to be split into self contained 3-car trains. These converted cars became known as 'Control Trailers' and eventually nearly half the trailer fleet was so converted.

Although the CLR had not originally claimed to have aspirations towards expansion some ideas in this direction had been spawned by the practical problems found with locomotive operation. Difficulties had soon been identified at terminal stations where it was necessary to uncouple the engine at the leading end of the train and couple either the same or another engine at the other end. Even after a year or so of practice it proved impossible to cut down this ritual to under 2¼ minutes, and even then the staff were hard pushed; this effectively limited the maximum service to 24 trains an hour. Prior to the adoption of multiple-unit operation the CLR actively considered constructing reversing loops at both ends of the line to overcome these problems – they had seen a similar system in use in Paris. Although a Bill was prepared for the 1901 Session, the Parliamentary process slowed it down and it was withdrawn. A

One of the new motor cars at Wood Lane depot in 1903. The power house is in the background and some of the overhead wires are also visible, although it was not much later that conductor rails were laid. *M.A.C.Horne collection*

more ambitious proposal was then formulated whereby the existing CLR would become the north side of a tube level circle line, the remainder of which would run via Liverpool Street, back to Bank and thence via Queen Victoria Street, Fleet Street, Strand, Piccadilly, Knightsbridge, Kensington Road, Hammersmith and Goldhawk Road to an end on junction with the existing railway at Shepherds Bush. Because of the number of tube railway bills being promoted at the time, the CLR Bill went before a special Select Committee of the House of Lords which, ultimately, rejected the scheme. Attempts to revive the scheme in later sessions were equally unsuccessful.

An extension which did proceed was at the western end of the line to serve the site reserved for the huge Franco-British exhibition. The extension, authorized in July 1907, was built largely on existing CLR land and was in the form of a loop line. The existing single track depot access road from Shepherds Bush became the new 'down' line and part of the depot was re-arranged to accommodate the new station, which consisted of two platforms either side of the curved new loop line. Beyond these platforms a new 'up' line was constructed which dived down and joined the end of an existing siding just west of Shepherds Bush. This arrangement resulted partly from the constraints of the existing depot and tunnel layout and partly in order to avoid needlessly introducing another very sharp curve such as already existed under Caxton Road; the practical effect of this was that trains operated around the loop in an anti-clockwise direction. The new station came into use on 14th May 1908, the day that the new exhibition opened. There was not a great deal of residential development in the area and the traffic here was based largely on that interchanging with the trams and the special traffic resulting from this and subsequent exhibitions. The Metropolitan Railway also opened a station at Wood Lane, but there was no connection with the CLR.

The twopenny flat fare lasted until the end of June 1907 when a threepenny fare was introduced for journeys longer than seven or eight stations. From the same date through bookings were introduced with the new Bakerloo and Hampstead tube railways (physical connections already existed for interchange purposes but passengers had previously been expected to re-book, special ticket offices having been built for this purpose). Penny fares were also introduced from March 1909 and season tickets became available from July 1911. The similarity in the service offered by the various tube railways was exploited from 1908/9 by the adoption by nearly all of them of a marketing device using the word UNDERGROUND with large initial and final letters and a narrow bar above and below the other letters. This was applied to station entrances to promote a common image and at about the same time a joint map was produced for use on the respective companies' publicity. Prior to this the CLR had used signs outside its own stations displaying the word TUBE — a word which was thereafter frowned upon for use in publicity, although stubbornly refusing to go away in its use by the public.

In 1909 it became possible to dispense with the assistant drivers following the introduction of two particular safety devices. One of these was automatic trainstop apparatus installed at the stop signals. This comprised a small lever next to the track which was raised when the associated signal was at danger. When raised, this lever engaged with an arm on the train connected to the braking system via a 'tripcock' valve. Thus a train which attempted to pass a signal at danger would be brought to a rapid halt by the emergency brake operating. A further safety device was also provided whereby the master controller handle had constantly to be kept depressed by the driver; in the event of it being released — if the driver were taken ill, for example — then the emergency brake would operate.

Although powers for extension of the line to Liverpool Street had lapsed, interest in this objective had remained and a new Act was passed in August 1909. Construction soon proceeded and the extension opened on 28th July 1912. The existing twin sidings

Interior of the signal cabin at Liverpool Street at about the time of the opening of the extension. *M.A.C.Horne collection*

beyond Bank were projected in a north-easterly direction to the new station where two platforms were provided. The line then continued beyond into two new siding tunnels. Crossover tunnels were built at each end of the platforms with a 'scissors' crossover arrangement in each. These crossovers were novel in that the diamond crossings in both crossover layouts used moveable switches. The extension was similar in appearance to the existing CLR although it proved possible to use bull-head track on conventional sleepers.

Liverpool Street station was the first on the Central Line to make use of that relatively new device – the escalator. Three inclined shafts were driven to receive these machines which would run from a point between the two platforms to a ticket hall beneath the Great Eastern Railway station. In the event up and down escalators were installed and the centre shaft received a fixed stairway, although an escalator could have been installed subsequently if required. These machines were not quite the first on the Underground but the station was the first to be opened where escalators were intended to be the main mode of access from the beginning (and even so, the working shaft was strategically placed for the installation of lifts if the escalators proved a disaster!). In the absence of a combed tread these early escalators involved the use of a 'shunt' landing at the disembarking end where passengers had to step off sideways. The 'up' machine allowed people to step directly on board at the lower end and was not reversible while the down machine could be reversed if necessary, requiring a shunt arrangement at top and bottom. Additional escalators were introduced on 10th October 1912 to link the CLR platforms with Broad Street (North London Railway) station although lifts were also introduced in February 1913 in view of the very large vertical distance from the CLR platforms to the North London Railway concourse.

The mechanical signalling on the CLR proved to be a major obstacle in improving the service, despite the number of block sections being significantly increased. At the time the railway opened there was no automatic system deemed suitable for use in a tube environment, but by 1910 such systems had become an established and proven success on several underground lines. Inevitably, the CLR came to make the decision to introduce automatic signals and the contract went to McKenzie, Holland & Westinghouse, the new signalling coming into use between 1912 and 1914. The existing signal boxes were closed except at Wood Lane, Queens Road, Marble Arch, British Museum and Bank. At these stations the signal boxes, frames and mechanical point connections were retained. Coloured light signals were substituted for mechanical signals and the frames were adapted to suit this method of operation. The very much simplified track layout at Shepherds Bush made the old mechanical frame redundant and an 11-lever power frame with miniature levers was introduced in 1913 to control the signals and trailing crossover there. Except at the terminal stations it was arranged that when the sidings or crossovers were not required the individual signal boxes could be closed and the coloured light signals would operate completely automatically.

The entire line was equipped with track circuits and except where the signal cabins were retained the signals operated quite automatically. Because the running rails were also used for returning the traction current the use of 'impedance bonds' was required – these allowed traction current to pass across the block section insulation but prevented the a.c. signal current from doing so. Generally, two-aspect coloured light signals were installed with some of the stop signals provided with repeaters where sighting was awkward. At Wood Lane, in the open air, two of the stop signals were of upper quadrant semaphore type, each controlled by an electro-pneumatic mechanism. Each of the stop signals was equipped with an air-operated trainstop and all coloured light signals were of the 'flux-neutralizer' type where the need for some of the relays otherwise required was obviated by what can best be described as a primitive form of solid state circuitry. The Liverpool Street extension opened with automatic signals in use from the start and the signal frame was a 12-lever electro-pneumatic type with miniature levers, all pointwork being controlled by compressed air.

The CLR was unusual among the tube companies in operating a parcels delivery service from 1911. Parcels were collected and delivered to and from the CLR stations by boys on bicycles and were conveyed in special compartments on the trains where they were also sorted. The service lasted until 1917.

The working life of the Central London Railway as an independent concern was not a very long one, being under thirteen years. During this time it had been both a technical and a commercial success. In the next period of its history it was no less valuable in serving London but its development was modified by its loss of independence and an increasing requirement to work as an adjunct to a combination of other services. These circumstances arose when the Central London Railway shareholders were persuaded that their financial interests would be better served under the umbrella of the same holding company responsible for running a number of other underground railways in London, and on 1st January 1913 the Central London Railway became part of the group of companies operated by the Underground Electric Railways Company of London Limited (UERL). The CLR directors resigned and were replaced by nominees from the UERL, and for the next twenty years the CLR was worked as a component of a network of transport services which included bus and tramway services as well as other underground lines. The process of consolidation took a major leap forward in 1915 when a statutory revenue pool was introduced and the various component railways became effectively managed as a single concern.

Before the UERL had assumed control of the CLR, the latter railway had been actively examining two possible extensions to the west, and the new management initially continued to show interest in furthering these schemes. One of these proposals involved a new tube line to Gunnersbury although it was not until the company was under UERL control that the Parliamentary powers were actually obtained. The necessary Act was passed on 15th August 1913 and authorized a new railway from a point just west of Shepherds Bush station (where new junctions would be built), thence via the Goldhawk Road and south-westwards to surface just to the east of Gunnersbury station on the London & South Western Railway, whence it was intended to exercise running powers to Richmond. Had not the First World War broken out then perhaps something

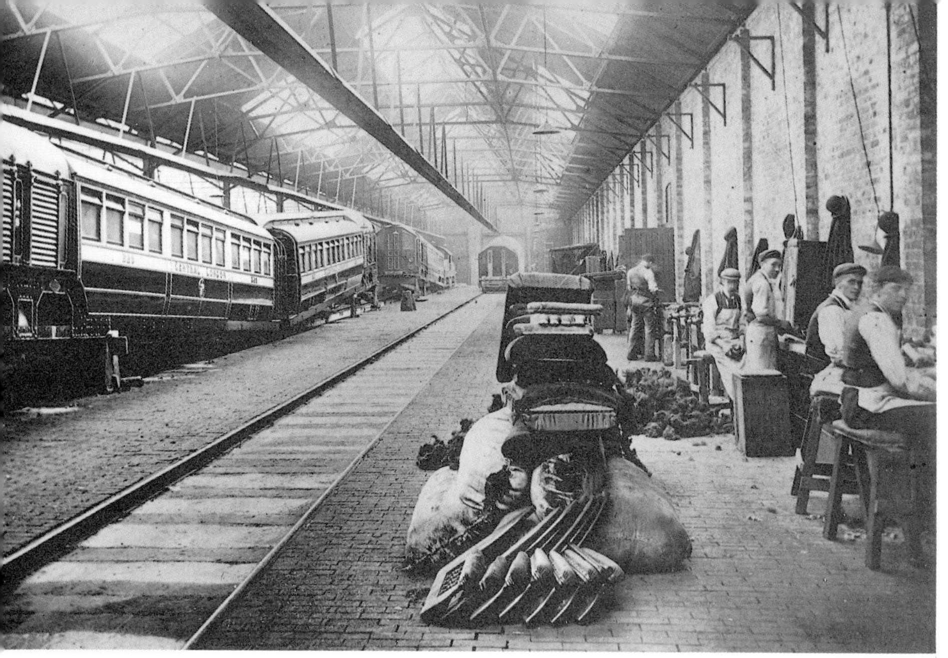

View of the workshops at Wood Lane depot after 1903 showing motor cars under repair.
J.Liffen collection

of this scheme would have materialized, but by the end of the war the position was such that other UERL schemes were now viable and their history is better dealt with elsewhere.

The second proposal involved the Great Western Railway (GWR) which had obtained in 1905 an Act authorizing the construction of a new length of line known as the Ealing & Shepherds Bush railway (E&SB). This was to run from a junction with the West London Railway from a point north of Uxbridge Road to a junction with its existing main line at Ealing. Although the GWR had intended to build a station at Shepherds Bush, the new line passed fairly close to Wood Lane (CLR) station and in 1911 the CLR had obtained Parliamentary authority to build a short link from Wood Lane to the proposed E&SB line; from this new junction it was intended to exercise running powers to Ealing Broadway. Although construction started in 1912 the E&SB works were severely restricted because of the First World War and did not open until April 1917 when a GWR freight service began. Work was later carried out to electrify the line, construct the stations and install automatic signalling. This completed, a passenger service, provided entirely by the CLR, began on 3rd August 1920.

The E&SB was a double-track line throughout, and was partly in cutting and partly on embankment. Stations were provided initially at East Acton (platforms flanking the tracks) and Ealing Broadway where a pair of terminal tracks flanked an island platform and the new lines were squeezed between the existing GWR and District Railway stations. The electric power for the E&SB was obtained from the GWR power station at Park Royal and fed from a substation at Old Oak Common (about half-way between East Acton and North Acton Junction). Both installations were already in use and supplying power to the Hammersmith & City Railway.

The GWR had experimented with three position semaphore signals at Paddington in 1914 and decided to adopt a similar pattern of signals on the E&SB. The running signals, which were electrically operated, were therefore designed to show three aspects, being Clear, Caution and Stop — the semaphore arm being, respectively, vertically upright, sloping upwards and horizontal (although not every signal could show all three aspects). All stop signals were provided with a trainstop mechanism. An additional feature was the provision of coloured light 'fog repeating' signals in advance of the stop signals — as the name suggests, these were switched on in foggy weather and repeated the indication of the next signal, a green light repeating the clear indication and yellow repeating either caution or danger. The signal frame at North Acton was of the mechanical type with the crossover connections with the GWR mechanically operated and the points fitted with locking bars. At Wood Lane Junction a mechanical frame was also provided but only the facing points were mechanically operated (though locked by track circuit) — the trailing connection was made using spring points. At Ealing Broadway an electro-pneumatic frame with miniature levers was employed, and was erected in an enlarged District Railway signal cabin; here, the points were operated by compressed air.

A new (electro-pneumatic) miniature frame was also installed at Wood Lane station, where some interesting alterations were made in order to accommodate the link with the E&SB line. As mentioned earlier, the existing station at Wood Lane consisted of a single-track loop line with a platform each side and around which trains travelled in an anti-clockwise direction. The link with the E&SB had therefore to be made by connecting the new tracks to points on each side of the loop, necessarily avoiding the existing platforms and requiring changes to depot access tracks. New platforms were therefore required on the new up and down lines to serve trains on the Ealing service and the station was expanded accordingly. One result of the chosen arrangement at Wood Lane was that the tracks towards Ealing incorporated right-hand running. Since the E&SB adopted the customary left-hand running arrangement it was necessary for the lines to cross over one another by means of a flyover at Wood Lane Junction, where CLR trains joined the line from the West London Railway. This flyover is still in use today.

A train of CLR stock at Wood Lane depot following reconstruction of the cars for provision of air-operated doors. The motor cars received a single doorway per car side, equipped with double doors, while the trailers received two single doorways per car side. This particular car has had the hinged cab-front doors altered to slide open and still retains the right-hand driving position. Behind the train is the power house building. *UERL official photograph* *

Through tickets to CLR stations were issued at Ealing and East Acton, but since the E&SB line was part of the GWR the fares charged for the portion of the journey from Ealing to Wood Lane were based on the GWR scale of fares rather than the cheaper scale of the CLR. The new route became popular very quickly for journeys to the West End and City and service levels were soon improved. In addition, two new stations were soon built – West Acton and North Acton, both opened on 5th November 1923 and both of a somewhat low-key character. At North Acton new platforms were also built on the adjacent GWR Wycombe Line, and a footbridge linked them all together.

Additional rolling stock was needed to cope with the extension of CLR services to Ealing and in 1915 Brush Engineering delivered 24 new motor cars for this purpose. The delay to the opening of the line caused these cars to be stored initially, but many of them briefly found a use on the Bakerloo Line prior to employment on the CLR in 1920. The cars were the first on the Underground to do away with the gated end entrances, which were now fully enclosed and fitted with doors giving access to the platform – doors were also installed in the centre of the cars. The new vehicles were also equipped with a more advanced system of multiple-unit control

View of a 1914 motor car near Ealing after provision of air-worked doors. The new carbody structure may be noted together with the new motor bogie. *Photomatic Limited*

whereby the starting resistances were automatically cut out of the circuit when the master controller was moved to the 'series' or 'parallel' positions. This made them incompatible with the existing motor cars and thus the CLR effectively became operated by two types of train known as 'Ealing' stock (trains incorporating the new cars) and 'Tunnel' stock (those comprising the old motor cars). Existing trailer cars, otherwise surplus to requirements, were modified to work with the new motor cars. In due course there proved to be insufficient of the Ealing stock to meet service requirements and eight 'tunnel' type motor cars and further trailers were converted to be compatible with the existing Ealing stock.

Apart from the large number of staff required to operate each train, one of the main problems with the old gate-ended cars was the length of time required for all the passengers to get on and off at stations. As the passenger traffic grew so the problem of boarding times became more acute. Following the success of sliding, air-operated doors on some cars on other lines, it was decided to fit

Brush built car of 1914 vintage intended for use on the Ealing extension. Photograph believed taken at the manufacturer's works prior to delivery. *M.A.C.Horne collection*

similar doors on a CLR trailer in 1924 to assess the difficulties which would be involved in modifying the whole fleet. The experiment was considered a great success and the decision was made to modernize the whole of the CLR rolling stock.

The work involved was fairly extensive and was contracted out to another Underground Group subsidiary, the Union Construction Company (UCC), which built and occupied premises in Feltham in order to carry out the work. The tenancy of the UCC site was actually taken by the CLR in December 1925 and then assigned to the UCC, the CLR guaranteeing the rent. All the 1900-1903 cars were completely updated and the internal layout re-arranged to provide for vestibule areas where the new doorways were to be. The bodywork was adjusted to allow for one door per car side on the motor cars and two doors per car side on the trailers. On the trailers the two doorways were spaced at one-third and two-thirds the way along the cars and the gate ends were dismantled and the car ends completely enclosed with additional windows and seats provided. The motor car ends were also enclosed but a swing door was provided for the use of the guard – of whom two per 6-car train were retained (the Gatemen, of course, being dispensed with). The Ealing stock motor cars were also modernized but in a fairly drastic way. The existing steel-panelled body was removed behind the switch compartment and replaced by a wooden structure similar in appearance to the modernized 1903 cars.

Meanwhile, modernization of the CLR stations and structures had been found necessary too. The Underground Group had taken a dim view of the idiosyncratic CLR track and almost immediately after taking over had begun the long and weary task of replacing the bridge rail and longitudinal timbers with bull-head rail and cross sleepers – a job soon delayed by the First World War and not finished for over twenty years. The CLR lifts were also adjusted to suit UERL practice, initially by fitting the exit doors with an air-operating mechanism and, later, by fitting controllers at the landings to enable two staff to control a number of lifts between them. At several busy stations the lifts were superseded by escalators and between 1924 and 1926 they were introduced at Bank (May 1924), Shepherds Bush (November 1924), Oxford Circus CLR (July 1925), Tottenham Court Road (February 1926) and Bond Street (June 1926). Post Office station was enlarged in 1929 but although powers were obtained in 1931 for installation of escalators there the work was not carried out for a few years more and they did not come into use until January 1939. Marble Arch received escalators in August 1932 and Chancery Lane in June 1934. At Post Office (renamed St Paul's in 1937) and Chancery Lane new sub-surface ticket halls were built a little way from the old top stations while at

Marble Arch station in 1938 showing night workers in the process of substituting standard bull-head rails (in the foreground) for the old CLR bridge rail on longitudinal timbers.
LPTB official photograph *

Tottenham Court Road a subway linked the disused CLR station building with the existing sub-surface ticket hall of what is now the Northern Line.

The power station at Wood Lane managed to keep pace with the developing railway until 1928, when the UERL began to supply the CLR from the massive power station at Lots Road and closed the Wood Lane establishment – a useful economy measure completing a plan originally formulated before the First World War. In due course part of the building was used to house a new substation. New high-tension feeder cables were installed from Lots Road power station to the Wood Lane substation, from where power was distributed to Notting Hill Gate and Bond Street substations. At the east end of the line Post Office substation was closed down and low-tension power was taken from the Piccadilly Line substation at Russell Square and the District Railway substation at Mansion House, via switch houses at Holborn (feeding the track at British Museum) and Bank respectively.

While the CLR passed above the Piccadilly Line near the latter's Holborn station there was no physical connection between the two railways and the nearest CLR station was British Museum, nearly two hundred yards distant and across two busy roads. The demand for interchange was one of some long standing and was acknowledged by the issuing of through tickets via this route. In 1930 an Act was obtained to allow for the complete rebuilding of Holborn station and for the enlarged station to cater for CLR traffic as well. New, large diameter platform tunnels were therefore excavated around the existing CLR running tunnels, which were later dismantled to allow the platforms to be built. The resulting station consisted of a flight of four escalators leading from ticket hall level to a lower concourse from which stairs led to the new CLR platforms and further escalators to the Piccadilly Line. The new CLR platforms and final pair of escalators opened on 25th September 1933 and British Museum station closed the previous day (although the signal cabin and siding remained in use there when required).

The position of the terminal loop at Wood Lane, and the necessary connections to and from the depot, severely restricted the length of the loop platforms which were initially adequate only for six cars. The need for 7-car trains demanded longer platforms and the 'outer' platform was lengthened at the approach end, although this brought it beyond the depot points. The longer platform was used for alighting traffic, and the shorter one for those boarding (with no access to the rear car). With increasing traffic levels this arrangement was not satisfactory and it was decided to extend the shorter 'inner' platform. As such lengthening would foul the track leading to the depot it was decided to make the platform extension moveable so that it could be swung out of the way when a depot train was run – this was achieved by an electro-pneumatic mechanism controlled from the signal box and was fully interlocked with the signalling. The arrangement was introduced in 1928 and lasted until the station was closed.

The year 1933 was a notable one for other reasons though. On 1st July, after years of public debate, a new type of public authority came into being. This was the London Passenger Transport Board (LPTB), which took over the responsibility for all London's bus, underground railway and tramway services. A noteworthy factor was that the Chairman and Vice-Chairman of the new Board were no lesser individuals than Lord Ashfield and Frank Pick who had previously been Chairman and Managing Director, respectively, of the UERL. The headquarters of the LPTB was Holden's impressive 55 Broadway complex in Westminster which had previously been the headquarters of the UERL and constituent companies – whose staff in any case formed the bulk of the new LPTB employees. It is not surprising, therefore, that no major changes of policy happened very quickly. Nevertheless, part of the justification for the new Board was the increased opportunity for further schemes of expansion and co-ordination.

The formation of the London Passenger Transport Board was not an event merely incidental to the expansion of the Central London Line (as the CLR became known under the new regime). Official disquiet about the state of the rail transport facilities east of Liverpool Street existed before the First World War and the demand for something better became more vociferous in the early 'twenties. The generally unsatisfactory nature of the facilities was exemplified partly by the huge interchange traffic between the Great Eastern and Central London Railway, and partly by the manifest lack of capacity of Liverpool Street (GER) station and its approaches in coping with the prevailing traffic, at least while using steam traction.

Matters had received official note when a public inquiry by the London & Home Counties Traffic Advisory Committee took place in 1926. The thrust of their report was that electrification of the Great Eastern suburban lines (by now under LNER control) to Chingford, Ongar and Shenfield would do much to ease travelling conditions, and that not very much was likely to happen without some alteration in the political climate such that there was more incentive for the main line railways and the Underground Group to work together. A common fund system was suggested, such as already existed within the UERL. The following year the Chairman of the LNER explained to the Minister of Transport that they had abandoned the idea of making certain improvements at Stratford and that for the present they were not going to embark on electrification because of the cost (while electrification would undoubtably have improved conditions the LNER argued it would not bring in adequate **additional** revenue to pay for the investment). The question of a government contribution was broached but the Minister's response was that such a precedent could not possibly be contemplated. The Chairman of the LNER stated that he hoped that an extension of the Underground east of Liverpool Street might be considered in order to relieve the most overcrowded areas, particularly in Ilford, and he proposed to draw this possibility to the attention of the UERL.

The Traffic Advisory Committee reports were just one, albeit a significant one, of the factors which resulted in the eventual formation of the LPTB. However, the demand for co-ordination with the main line companies was not overlooked, and with the LPTB came a statutory pooling scheme of the revenues both of the new Board and of the main line railways within the Board's area — adminis-

One of the surviving CLR locomotives, probably about 1930, showing the geared motor trucks of 1901/2 design. *M.A.C.Horne collection*

tered by a standing joint committee which became the *de facto* public transport planning authority. The door was now open for co-ordination on a scale seen neither before nor since.

An early result of the London Passenger Transport Pool was the production of a report in December 1933 discussing transport problems in north-east London and making proposals. It set down on paper a carefully considered plan based on the 1926/27 thinking, namely electrification of LNER suburban lines from Liverpool Street and Fenchurch Street to Ongar and Shenfield (on the then standard 1500 volt d.c. overhead wire system), and the independent extension of the Central London Line from Liverpool Street via Mile End and north Ilford to a terminus at Little Heath, beneath the Eastern Avenue a little to the north of Goodmayes. The report stated that the Central London Line extension was deliberately designed to compete with the LNER lines to relieve traffic (with the Pooling system in operation there would have been no net revenue loss to the LNER). The report also noted that the Pool could not in any way afford to finance the scheme. "The Statutory Standing Joint Committee of the London Passenger Transport Board and the main line railways can, therefore, only state this problem in its broad bearings and submit it for the consideration of the Minister of Transport".

Considerable negotiation with the government took place during the following year during which time the proposal was simplified (made less expensive) by adjusting the route of the new tube line in certain places. The result was a proposal to electrify at least part of the Ongar branch on the 600 volt d.c. conductor rail system and make connections with the new tube at Leyton and Leytonstone, with the eastern terminus diverted from Little Heath to plug into the Fairlop loop line instead. The Shenfield electrification was still planned on the 1500 volt overhead basis. The financial arrangements were complicated because even by 1935 public transport was not seen as an area to which public money could just be handed by the government. The Central London Line extension was embodied in a substantial scheme of new works, affecting nearly every line (and many road services), which the government was prepared to assist by the establishment of a statutory finance corporation to raise the money through shares, which would be backed by government guarantee. The scheme became known as the 1935-40 New Works Programme.

The history of the Ongar branch and Fairlop loop are worthy of examination as they were to become an important component of the London Underground, if not one of the oldest components. It was under the ownership of the Eastern Counties Railway that the line from Loughton Branch Junction (near Stratford) opened to Loughton in August 1856. The line was double track and stations were provided at Low Leyton (now Leyton), Leytonstone, Snaresbrook, George Lane (now South Woodford), Woodford, Buckhurst Hill and Loughton, where the terminus was situated in the High Street. The intermediate stations have all been subject to varying degrees of reconstruction and some have been at least partly resited. The Eastern Counties Railway became part of the Great Eastern in 1862. The Loughton terminus was not long lived; a single-track extension line was opened in April 1865 from a point a little to the south of the Loughton terminus to Ongar. A new station serving Loughton was provided on the new alignment and the 1856 terminus was abandoned. Other intermediate stations were built at Chigwell Road (later Chigwell Lane), Theydon (later Theydon Bois), Epping, North Weald and Blake Hall. Epping and later Theydon Bois were passing places but the line between Loughton and Epping became double track in 1893.

The Fairlop loop line was opened by the Great Eastern in May 1903 and linked the Loughton branch from a point a little north of Woodford to the Southend line by means of a triangular junction at Seven Kings. Intermediate stations were built at Chigwell, Grange Hill, Hainault, Barkingside, Fairlop and Newbury Park (Roding Valley was added in 1936).

Another part of the New Works Programme was the proposal to

widen the GWR line from North Acton to Ruislip and construct two new tracks, electrified to allow Central London Line trains to use them. This section of the Great Western system was administered by the GWR (Old Oak Common to South Ruislip) and the Great Western and Great Central Joint Committee (South Ruislip to West Ruislip and beyond). It opened in the early years of this century and stations were largely of the 'halt' (stop on request) status. Although traffic had been very slow to develop a large number of factories had emerged after the First World War, and it was considered that a frequent electric train service would be the best way of serving both this traffic and that from the expanding residential development. The initial proposal was to construct the new electric tracks to the main line loading gauge with a long term view of projecting District Line trains from Ealing Broadway to West Ruislip line via the GWR's Castlebar loop. Although this service projection was not pursued before the war, all work on the Ruislip extension was executed to main line standards and this aided some temporary main line track diversions while the work was in progress.

The substantial additional traffic likely to result from the whole of the new works was to be catered for by lengthening the existing platforms, some central area station reconstruction and new, more modern rolling stock. Provision was made for all these as a part of the programme. It would be helpful here to say that the Central London Line was renamed the Central Line in 1937, and it is convenient to use this, shorter, title from this point onwards.

Most of the Parliamentary powers for the Central Line extensions were granted in 1936 and contracts for tunnelling on the Mile End to Leyton section were awarded in October that year, some haste being evident in view of the anticipated trouble in tunnelling through water-bearing ground. Many of the major contracts were awarded in 1937 for works at both east and west ends of the line and the remaining major contracts were let in 1938. Progress on these extensive works was fairly rapid and by February 1938 it was anticipated that the Central Line would be extended to Stratford by summer 1940 and Newbury Park by December 1940.

In 1937 the LPTB put forward proposals for additional works to be added to the main programme. Amongst others this involved a further westwards extension, from West Ruislip to Denham, and further electrification at the east end of the line from Loughton to Ongar; the purpose of the latter was simply in order to displace the proposed steam shuttle service which was now considered likely to be an operational inconvenience. It was also considered expedient to quadruple the tracks between Wood Lane Junction and North Acton Junction in order to completely segregate the Central Line and GWR goods services. Reconstruction of the operationally difficult station at Wood Lane was also envisaged, together with those at Liverpool Street, Tottenham Court Road and Notting Hill Gate. The re-introduction of lifts at Oxford Circus was also planned. Although the source of finance for all this additional work (about £5,000,000) was not finally agreed, work was started nevertheless. In fact the Great Western had moved so quickly that the additional goods tracks along the E&SB were ready in June 1938, and the existing junctions had been removed.

The extension east of Liverpool Street involved substantial reconstruction of the east end of the platforms, sidings and crossover tunnels there, and two reversing sidings were retained with the new tracks running either side of them. A new station was to be built at Bethnal Green with the tunnels continuing to Mile End where cross-platform interchange with the District Line was intended. Stratford LNER station was to be substantially rebuilt and the Central Line tracks would surface here to provide cross-platform interchange with the to-be-electrified Shenfield services. Beyond Stratford the Central Line would dive into tunnel again to emerge just south of Leyton station where it would meet the LNER line to Loughton. The LNER would electrify the Loughton branch, provide various new facilities and resignal the line to LPTB standards. At Leytonstone a new junction would be formed and a pair of tube tunnels would carry a branch of the Central Line beneath Eastern Avenue, through stations at Wanstead, Redbridge and Gants Hill to a junction with the LNER Ilford to Woodford loop line at Newbury Park. This loop line via Fairlop to Woodford would also be electrified and a new depot would be built at Hainault to service the stock needed to operate the much extended tube railway.

While the LPTB was embarking on major extension at both ends of the Central Line, the original section from Wood Lane to Liverpool Street, with worn out trains and equipment, received no less attention. New trains were a major priority. Prototypes were built and tested on the Piccadilly Line and embodied a new feature for tube stock — the motor bogies and control equipment were all below floor level, which significantly increased the space for passenger accommodation. The lines needing additional tube-type trains were the Northern, Bakerloo and Central, but the latter two had existing platform lengths suitable only for 6-car trains and would require lengthening at all costs. The Northern had platforms long enough for seven cars and after deliberation the Board concluded that the Northern could get by with 7-car trains of the new type. So the Central Line's projected new stock went to the Northern (and Bakerloo) Line and the Northern Line's existing trains, dating from 1923-27, were earmarked for the Central.

Before any 'modern' trains could operate various problems had to be overcome. The current collection system was of the 'third-rail' earthed return type, not standard with the rest of the system. Furthermore, the tunnels and track conspired to make the addition of a positive rail in the usual position a very difficult task. After some investigation it was decided that a fourth-rail system would be proceeded with. This involved a certain amount of track re-alignment and the laying of large amounts of positive rail of a unique inverted 'L' section which would not foul the tunnel wall; to increase the conductivity a copper strip was bonded to the underside. Even despite these measures the new rail was about an inch higher than the LPTB standard and, even today, requires the shoegear on trains to be adjusted to accommodate the higher lift. The second problem was the tight gauge of the tunnels for modern trains. Without the concrete lining the tunnels were a nominal 11ft 8¼ ins internal diameter. However numerous imperfections of level and line and of the junction work between different tunnel drives made the practical gauge in many places rather smaller. A huge programme was thus started of adjusting the line of the tunnel, involving work on and behind some 10,000 segments, all during the brief non-traffic hours. The result was tunnels through the central area which were suitable for the new trains to operate at fairly high speed.

Allied with the tunnel reconstruction was the problem of platform lengthening. In essence this meant excavating beyond the platform end, extending the existing station tunnel, removing the segments around the old running tunnel and then laying in the permanent new trackbed and platform. The task was made much more complicated because the old CLR stations had been built on a hump, with a 1 in 60 approach and a 1 in 30 departure gradient, to assist trains in slowing down and speeding up at stations. It was not desired to have platforms on gradients as steep as this which meant a considerable amount of extra work had to be done in adjusting the level of the line from a point some way away from the actual platform extension work.

Considering the amount of work involved the tunnel reconstruction work was progressed quickly and by September 1938 it was sufficiently advanced to allow the trains displaced from the Northern Line to start coming into service on the Central, operating in 6-car formations. One problem was that the 4-rail current collection system was not ready and the trains had to be temporarily modified for 3-rail operation (the conventional positive shoegear was removed and the wires bonded to the bogie frames). The last of the old trains was displaced in July 1939. Most of the platform extension work and the last of the new track were ready early the

Work in progress in 1937 showing the tunnel enlargement and re-alignment process. The miner in the foreground is cutting away a veneer of clay, while packing pieces, for increasing the effective diameter of the tunnel, can be seen between the right-hand segments. *LPTB official photograph* *

following year.

On 21st April 1940 the new 4-rail current collection system came into use following a huge equipment change-over the previous night. For the previous few weeks the trains had gradually been fitted with new shoegear for collecting current from the new outside rails, but this was not connected up until the change-over. Following the change, the negative side of the traction supply system was entirely isolated from earth, which allowed the last stages of the re-signalling scheme to be undertaken.

The new signalling was introduced between Shepherds Bush and a point east of Bank in several stages in the latter half of 1940, and was designed to cater for a much increased train service. Automatic signalling was installed throughout this section except at Queens Road (existing signal box retained), Marble Arch (existing signal box retained), Holborn (new signal box with electro-pneumatic frame controlling British Museum siding — British Museum signal box closed) and Bank (existing signal box retained). A new signal cabin had already been brought into use at Liverpool Street in 1937.

A 7-car train of 1923-27 stock near Northolt in 1956. *Photomatic Limited*

While the modernization of the central area of the Central Line was largely completed, the outbreak of the Second World War was an event which cast the impending extensions into some turmoil. After initially considering stopping work completely it was then proposed to pursue some of the works already in an advanced stage, and it was hoped to open the whole of the eastern extension as far as Loughton and the western extension as far as Greenford. When the war neared British shores in 1940 circumstances became very much more difficult. In early May 1940 it was intended to begin trial running from Liverpool Street eastwards on 1st October, with a view to opening the section to Loughton and Grange Hill (via Woodford) in November. But war conditions deteriorated so rapidly that tracklaying was suspended on 24th May and after urgent discussions with the Ministry the whole extension scheme was suspended from mid June, some minor works continuing in order to secure construction which could not be left unfinished.

By this time some of the tunnels in the Liverpool Street area had been considered for use as air raid shelters, to which use they were put in July 1940; in due course some of the new tunnels towards Stratford were put to similar use. Between Wanstead and Newbury Park the tunnels were later utilized as a temporary aircraft component factory, displacing a public shelter at Redbridge station. Much of the new track was lifted for use elsewhere, and on the western extension this amounted to nearly ten miles' worth. The Shenfield electrification had already been suspended and LNER steam trains continued to operate services on the Ongar branch and via the Fairlop loop until after the war. The depot sites at Ruislip and Hainault were both largely completed and were utilized for military purposes for the duration.

When war broke out the LPTB and main line companies were placed under government control in the form of the Railway Executive Committee, under whose control it remained until nationalization on 1st January 1948 when the Committee was superseded by the British Transport Commission. Under the Commission the LPTB and certain other lines were transferred to a subsidiary body called the London Transport Executive.

When the war was over the wartime conditions under which the Country was suffering improved only very slowly and, in particular, steel shortages were paramount and supply was regulated by the government. Nevertheless the Central Line extensions were given a very high priority by the Cabinet and work started almost immediately, starting off with the demolition of the various wartime fixtures which had established themselves in the new tunnels and stations. Modified signalling came into use at Liverpool Street on 12th October 1946, and on 4th December 1946 the Central Line was extended eastwards to Stratford, with trains continuing almost as far as Leyton in order to reverse. One of the problems slowing down further projection was the large amount of work needed to eliminate a number of level crossings on the line prior to electrification – road diversions across or beneath new bridges being required in each case.

Beyond Stratford, the Central Line was extended as far as Leytonstone on 5th May 1947. Woodford and Newbury Park (direct) were both reached on 14th December 1947, Hainault (from Newbury Park) on 31st May 1948, and Loughton on 21st November 1948. This batch of Central Line extensions was met by a gradual withdrawal of the corresponding LNER service to form steam-hauled shuttles linking the Central Line with the outlying termini at Epping and Ongar. The simultaneous extension to Newbury Park and Woodford was problematical as it became virtually impossible for the LNER to maintain a service between these two stations around the northern side of the loop. The LNER loop service was therefore replaced by a special LPTB bus service. A few empty Central Line trains did work between Newbury Park and Hainault depot via Grange Hill during this period but the line was virtually unsignalled. Temporary stabling sidings were also laid at Newbury Park.

The eastern extensions involved a number of new tube stations, which were built at Bethnal Green, Wanstead, Redbridge and Gants Hill, each consisting of a single platform on each track.

Greenford in 1961 showing a westbound Central Line train and, in the bay road, a diesel railcar on the Ealing–Greenford shuttle service. *Photomatic Limited*

Redbridge was so near the surface that cut-and-cover construction was used; here, surface access was gained simply by steps, but escalators were provided at the other stations. The existing LNER stations on the Loughton branch at Leyton, Leytonstone, Snaresbrook, George Lane (which became South Woodford), Woodford and Buckhurst Hill remained little changed, but a minimum of new facilities were added to suit the new services. Leytonstone was extensively rebuilt, with a new ticket hall and an additional platform, while Loughton was completely reconstructed with three tracks and four platform faces. Around the loop line stations existed at Roding Valley, Chigwell, Grange Hill, Hainault, Fairlop, Barkingside and Newbury Park. Again, most were little changed although quite a lot of work was done at Hainault, which gained a new platform. At Newbury Park a new bus station was built, with a copper covered roof, and with it was constructed a new station entrance – but finance was such that plans for the station were never completed and until very recently tickets were sold at a 'temporary' ticket office to one side of the new building.

New signal cabins were built at Bethnal Green, Leytonstone, South Woodford, Woodford, Loughton, Newbury Park and Hainault, where there were junctions, sidings or reversing points; in each case a miniature power frame was installed (except at South Woodford where a mechanical frame was put in). Some existing signal cabins were also retained and modernized, and some ground frames were provided, mainly for use in connection with steam-hauled goods train operation which was to continue. All other signalling was to the normal London Transport standard with additional distant signal disks for the use of goods trains. Electric current was supplied from substations at Bethnal Green, Bow, Leyton, Leytonstone, South Woodford, Roding Valley, Loughton, Hainault, Newbury Park and Redbridge. Power was taken from London Transport's newly modernized ex-LCC tramways power station at Greenwich, and controlled from a new control room at South Woodford.

The western extension involved the construction of independent, electrified, tracks between North Acton and West Ruislip. Stations were provided at Hanger Lane, Perivale, Greenford, Northolt, South Ruislip, Ruislip Gardens and West Ruislip, in each case island platforms were built between the tracks. Greenford was reached on 30th June 1947. West Ruislip was reached on 21st November 1948 (the same date as for Loughton). Many of the stations were not entirely finished when opened and some temporary structures were built, notably at Hanger Lane where much delay was caused by discussions about a neighbouring road intersection. The existing halt at Park Royal had closed in 1937, but Park Royal West, Brentham and Perivale remained until the Central Line's better sited stations rendered them unnecessary in 1947 (the new station at Perivale was adjacent). At Greenford the new station also served the old platforms which were retained until June 1963; in addition a bay road was squeezed in at the south end of the Central Line platforms to accommodate the Western Region shuttle service to Ealing Broadway via the Castlebar loop. At Northolt the Central Line station was built on the other side of the road bridge to the ex-GWR station, partly with the long term aim of building another ticket office at the west end of the platforms for the racecourse traffic, but this never came about; the GWR station was closed. At South Ruislip, Ruislip Gardens and West Ruislip (formerly Ruislip & Ickenham) the old joint line platforms were all retained.

New signal cabins were built at North Acton, Greenford (where there was a reversing siding), and West Ruislip which also controlled a 'slave' cabin at Ruislip Gardens. The signalling was otherwise automatic. An extensive new depot was commissioned between Ruislip Gardens and West Ruislip. Since the new stations at Greenford, South Ruislip, Ruislip Gardens and West Ruislip were linked to the existing main line stations they were operated by the GWR (or, later, British Railways Western Region) although the signal cabins were run by London Transport staff; the other stations were run entirely by London Transport. Traction current was supplied from new substations at Ruislip, Northolt, Greenford and

Brentham, and controlled remotely from the ex-GWR substation at Old Oak Common.

While the Central Line was thrusting forward at each end, attention again was focused towards the totally unsatisfactory arrangements which now existed at Wood Lane. The depot, once spacious, had become cramped and was full of very sharp curves which were quite unsuitable for modern trains; the intention was to transfer the heavy maintenance done here to the new depots on the extension lines and to re-arrange the site to provide for a small number of stabling sidings suitable for the new 8-car trains. Wood Lane station had become a rambling and inefficient place where the loop platform had trouble dealing with 7-car trains and could not easily be made to cope with those of 8 cars. The answer was to do away with the loop and build a new station a little to the north-west.

The new station was called White City, and it replaced Wood Lane station on 23rd November 1947. Initially just two platforms were available, together with a reversing siding (west of the new platforms) operated by temporary equipment on the platform. The new White City signal box came into use on 4th July 1948 and the new track layout consisting of three platform roads and four platform faces came with it. Further re-arrangements took place subsequently, with much of the old depot being taken out of use on 27th November 1948 and most of the new sidings being commissioned on 7th August 1949. The old automatic semaphore signalling west of White City had already been replaced in 1946 to a point just west of the new junction at North Acton, and standard colour light signals were installed. North Acton signal box, however, was arranged to be controlled remotely from the new cabin at White City. The signalling between North Acton and Ealing Broadway was replaced in 1948 and at the latter station the connection between the E&SB line and the ex-GWR main line was removed. Further alterations at Ealing took place in 1952 when a new signal cabin was built (also controlling the District Line station); this was novel in employing a 'slave' power frame controlled by a push-button panel elsewhere in the building.

Some considerable argument took place about the concept of electrification beyond Loughton, which was not part of the new works agreed in 1935 and the finance for which had not been finalized before the outbreak of war. In the event the development of housing estates in the area, and the fact that quite a lot of work had already been done, won the argument for extension — but not before the matter had reached Cabinet level where the observation was made that had not so much work already been done then the extension beyond Loughton would have been out of the question.

Although other forms of motive power were examined (and tested), steam locomotives were the mainstay of the Epping–Ongar shuttle service until electrification. This view shows the push-pull shuttle train in the charge of an F5 class tank locomotive in 1956, amid the rural setting of the branch. The conductor rails, laid before electrification was halted in 1940, can also be seen. *R.C.Riley*

Central Line trains reached Epping from 25th September 1949, with intermediate stations at Debden (previously Chigwell Lane) and Theydon Bois. New signal cabins were commissioned at Debden (where there were reversing sidings) and Epping. At this latter station electric trains generally reversed in one of the platforms while the steam-hauled shuttle service to Ongar used the other one. A ground frame was provided at Theydon Bois for operating the goods yard there, signalling being otherwise automatic. A new substation was also commissioned at Epping. Initially only a few through trains outside rush hours operated beyond Debden to Epping and the service was supplemented by a 2-car train shuttling between Loughton and Epping.

Although electric trains only reached as far as Epping it was deemed administratively inconvenient for British Railways to continue to operate the residual section to North Weald, Blake Hall and Ongar; this resulted in the stations, staff and line being transferred to London Transport control, and for practical purposes this rural piece of single-track railway became a part of the Central Line from the date it extended beyond Loughton. The battle to get the line electrified as far as Epping did not augur well for Ongar, hence the steam service continued to shuttle between these two

Epping station in the early 1950s. In the foreground is one of the Loughton–Epping shuttle trains composed of 1935 experimental stock. These trains initially entered service on Central Line shuttle services in 2-car sets in 1949. In later years a 1927 stock trailer was added to make a 3-car train and (later still) the trains were painted silver to match the new aluminium alloy trains then being delivered. The 1935 stock worked at various times on the Loughton–Epping, Woodford–Hainault and Epping–Ongar shuttles and was finally withdrawn from the Ongar service in 1966. The steam locomotive in the background is an ex-Great Eastern Railway class F5 and is operating the Epping–Ongar push-pull shuttle service. *Lens of Sutton*

stations for some years more – the locomotive and rolling stock being provided by the Eastern Region on LT's behalf. Nevertheless, after a few years operation, it became possible to make out a convincing argument that a form of 'light' electrification would be cheaper in the long term than hiring in the steam service. Current rails (largely already laid!) were duly connected up and a bare minimum of additional signalling was installed, which did include track circuits. On 16th November 1957 the steam service was withdrawn, and a shuttle service of electric trains began operating from Monday 18th November.

Prior to the war it had been the intention to build a new substation at Blake Hall but this was now out of the question (although the equipment had been delivered). The result was a 6·1 mile (9·8km) section of railway fed only at the Epping end, and electrically capable of supporting one 8-car or up to two 4-car trains at a time. The initial train service comprised a single 2-car train – or two such trains during the rush hour – running between Epping and Ongar (these shuttles were later increased to three and then four cars). The station at North Weald was equipped with a passing loop and signal box with mechanical frame, and a goods yard. Little alteration was made here and the semaphore signals were retained. At Blake Hall there existed only a single platform and the station building was virtually the **only** building within site, surrounded by open fields, but there was nevertheless a small goods yard. Ongar only had a single platform, too, but had a more extensive goods yard and signal box and a good supply of potential passengers. Here, too, much of the existing mechanical signalling was retained.

The Fairlop loop presented a problem in deciding exactly which trains should terminate where. In LNER days loop trains generally ran from Liverpool Street, via Fairlop, only as far as Woodford, and vice versa. Although the type of service was to be very different, the LPTB had also been reluctant to run trains all the way round the loop and had intended from the start to terminate trains at Hainault, both from the Newbury Park and Woodford directions. Through services from London to Hainault via Woodford were contemplated for a while, but the pressure for trains on the Loughton branch, and the doubtful traffic potential on the northern side of the loop, conspired to produce a Woodford–Hainault shuttle service (although a number of through trains operated from London to Grange Hill in order to reach Hainault Depot). A factor which might have changed all this was a pre-war plan to develop a major London airport at Fairlop, including its own station (between the old Fairlop and Barkingside stations); although the City of London Corporation had purchased the land and pursued the scheme after the war, the rapid expansion of Heathrow made it unnecessary and a temporary wartime airfield on the site was eventually closed and the land sold off.

As part of the 'additional' new works it had been the pre-war intention to extend beyond West Ruislip to Denham, with an intermediate station at Harefield Road, to serve new housing and industry (including the film industry). In fact almost no work had been done and after the war this section fell into the newly defined Green Belt area. Although fresh consideration was given to resuming work it clearly commanded a very low priority and was abandoned. A link was made between the London Transport system and the Western Region line north of West Ruislip for stock interchange purposes and this link was for many years used for the delivery of new LT rolling stock.

The rolling stock for the Central Line extensions had been displaced from the Northern Line by the early years of the war but the delay to the extensions meant that those cars not immediately needed had had to be stored, many of them in the open air. Because of this, extensive reconditioning was required at the main overhaul works at Acton before they could be used; even so, reliability was not what it might have been. The fleet consisted of Motor Cars, Control Trailers and Trailers marshalled initially into 6-car trains and from 1947 into 7 or 8-car trains. The 7-car trains predominated and utilized three motor cars while the 8-car trains had four motor cars – two of which faced each other in the middle of trains creating a huge gap between adjacent doorways and thus lengthening boarding times (in later years the trains were re-formed to avoid this). Traffic levels at the east end of the line rose very quickly and trains became very overcrowded but sufficient rolling stock was not available to allow more 8-car trains to run. The maximum number of trains per hour was limited by the congestion which became evident at Liverpool Street, particularly on the eastbound line, though matters were slightly eased in April 1948 when a system of speed-controlled signalling was introduced in order to allow trains approaching the platform to do so more closely together, thereby increasing the total capacity. An additional ticket hall and escalators from November 1950 also helped passenger movement at platform level.

The lack of capacity at the east end of the line was apparent as early as 1948 and mindful that the Central Line rolling stock was the oldest on the system consideration was given to the introduction of more modern tube stock from the early 1950s. In addition to being of higher capacity any new trains would be more reliable and would allow 8-car operation throughout. In those austere times such a luxury failed to materialize even though it was intended to save money by using existing trailer cars. Although complete re-stocking was postponed, it was nevertheless recognised that it would be essential in about 1960. In preparation for this, three prototype trains entered service on the Piccadilly Line in 1957/58 for evaluation. These were of a similar general style to the 1938 tube stock where the equipment was all under-floor but the main obvious difference was in the construction of the bodywork which (while retaining a steel underframe) was of an aluminium alloy and unpainted. A large order for new trains was made on the basis of experience of the experimental ones, the new fleet being known as the 1959 tube stock. At this stage these trains were intended for use only on the Piccadilly Line, but this displaced a few of that line's cars for use on the Central.

For the Central Line, the idea of reaping potential economies by using existing trailer cars, suitably modernized, continued to be pursued. A new design of motor car (now known as a Driving

A 4-car unit of the 1960 prototype stock at about the time of delivery. Only the driving motor cars were new, the trailers being of 1927 to 1931 vintage although extensively modernized. The stock had a brief life on the main section of the Central Line where they ran as three 8-car trains. From 1964 most cars were converted for operation on the Woodford—Hainault shuttle service as 4-car automatic trains in connection with Victoria Line experimental work (the automatic equipment was removed in 1987).

LTE official photograph *

Motor Car) emerged which employed four traction motors instead of the two used on all previous tube stock; this did away with the need for the Non-Driving Motor Car (NDM) used on 1959 stock, and envisaged a four (new) motor, four (old) trailer train with better acceleration and braking than the existing stock — which meant a better train service.

To test out this concept twelve such driving motors were ordered from Cravens Limited. The new cars were built in aluminium alloy on steel underframes and the exteriors were unpainted. The car body was of a new, contemporary style and the windows between the doorways were very much larger than on earlier trains and lacked the usual tilting quarterlights at the top, ventilation being by pull-open panels just above the windows (designed not to let in water from automatic washing machines). Inside the cars plastic finishes were employed and a slightly modified car layout was employed to increase the width of the doorway vestibules. Several different interior colour schemes were used to see which looked best for the production trains. The new cars were to be formed into three trains, each consisting of two 4-car units which themselves comprised two new motor cars flanking two old trailers. Each 4-car unit was equipped with a fully automatic coupler at each end and, for the first time on tube stock, units could couple together either

A westbound 1962 stock train on the former Ealing & Shepherds Bush line west of White City where the tracks cross over to change right-hand to left-hand running. The former GWR link to the West London Railway ran parallel to, and to the left of, these tracks, but housing has now been built on much of the site. *M.A.C.Horne*

way round (reflecting the possibility of units becoming turned round because of the existence of the Hainault loop). The trailer cars were comprehensively modernized for their new role, being modified by the provision of, among other things, complete rewiring, fitting of fluorescent lighting, compressors and repainting in silver-coloured paint. After extensive testing the new trains came into service in November 1960 and, whilst a clear improvement on the existing trains, themselves presented a curiously non-uniform mixture of old and new styles.

Events did not follow their anticipated course. The arrival of the 1959 stock on the Piccadilly Line allowed a quantity of that line's old cars to be transferred to the Central Line, augmenting that fleet and allowing all trains to be operated as 8-car trains. However the improvement was not enough to make the desired inroad into the congestion problem and for a variety of reasons relief was required rather more urgently than was likely if the new style of train was adequately developed. It therefore proved expedient to adopt the more rapid course of ordering a further batch of trains similar to the Piccadilly Line's 1959 stock, and, in the short term, to divert the outstanding 1959 stock to the Central Line until such time as its own batch of trains arrived. The Central required 8-car trains and additional NDMs were delivered with the 1959 stock to extend them from seven to eight cars. These particular NDMs remained on the Central when the 1959 stock was eventually sent to its rightful home on the Piccadilly Line, and were absorbed into the Central's new trains. These became known as 1962 tube stock. The 1959 stock was evident on the Central Line from early 1960 until mid 1964. The first 1962 stock train entered service on 12th April 1962 and the last of the 1923-34 period trains was withdrawn from the main portion of the Central towards the end of 1962 (although the shuttle services were operated by various odds and ends for a few years more).

Following the immediate post-war expansion of the Central Line little substantial work was undertaken, other than the completion of some of the 1935-40 works which had been left in a somewhat incomplete state and now demanded attention. The platform extensions had been left without finished surfacing and a programme of tiling was undertaken in the early 1960s to a standard similar to the rest of the platforms (except the eastbound platform extension at Marble Arch which was, for some reason, left unfinished). West Ruislip, Ruislip Gardens, South Ruislip and Northolt station buildings had been left in various stages of temporariness when the western extensions had opened and were completed in 1962. This work was done by British Railways (Western Region), as successors to the GWR, although Northolt was operated by London Transport.

The Western Region was also busy at Ealing Broadway from 1961. The result was a brand new station building and new steps to all platforms, more or less integrating the former Ealing & Shepherds Bush platforms with the rest of the station (the new WR station also took over responsibility for ticket issuing for the adjacent District Line trains and the District station building was closed). The rebuilt station was opened in 1965. The remaining E&SB stations had passed to London Transport ownership in 1948. In passing, it should be noted that London Transport assumed responsibility for staffing the four stations between Hanger Lane and West Ruislip which were still under Western Region control on 13th November 1967. This transfer included the substations other than Old Oak Common, which was transferred a few years later.

One pre-war scheme which had been held in abeyance after only a little work had been done was the reconstruction of Notting Hill Gate station. Capital investment restrictions prevented an early resumption but, ironically, a pressing road-widening scheme required the old stations to go and the work recommenced in 1956.

It involved the construction of a new ticket hall beneath the road surface, a triple bank of escalators to an intermediate level, a further bank to Central Line westbound platform level, and yet more down to the eastbound platform. From the intermediate level an interchange passage was built to the District and Circle Line platforms. A considerable amount of difficult work was involved but the new station opened on 1st March 1959, with some finishing work continuing into the following year. The improvements allowed the old, separate station buildings and the Central Line lifts to be closed. A new substation had already opened at Notting Hill Gate (in 1943) replacing the old CLR equipment and this also provided a feed for the District and Circle Lines. A new substation opened at Liverpool Street in 1966, replacing the existing switch-house at Bank.

Central Line signalling was substantially new and once the post-war extensions had been opened subsequent alterations were few. Nevertheless original CLR 'mechanical' frames still existed at Queensway (as Queens Road became in 1946), Marble Arch and Bank and between 1951 and 1958 these frames were replaced by miniature electro-pneumatic frames. The signal box at Bank lasted until October 1970 when the crossover there was taken out of commission while that at Queensway survived until July 1982 when the siding was taken out of use. The signal cabin at South Woodford was modernized in 1961 when the mechanical frame there was replaced by a power frame and the mechanically operated points controlling the entrance to the goods yard were converted to power operation. At North Acton the 'slave' cabin controlling the junction was modified in 1973 such that push-button operation from the signal box at White City replaced control by the White City lever frame, the new arrangement allowing the crossover at North Acton also to be controlled remotely. At Ealing Broadway modernization of the District Line signalling in 1974 resulted in the closure of the signal box there and control of the Central Line platforms was transferred to a push button panel at White City, although an automatic reversing facility at Ealing meant that the signalman did not normally intervene. In passing it might be mentioned that a trailing connection between the Central Line and the Western Region had been put in at Ealing Broadway in 1945 to replace the double junction, it became unsignalled in 1948 and was removed in 1972.

Little very major construction work took place on the Central Line in the 1960s, with the notable exception of the work at Oxford Circus necessitated by the building of the Victoria Line. The joint Central and Bakerloo Line station there had been hard pushed in dealing with prevailing traffic virtually from the day it opened in its enlarged form in 1925. A palliative was given in the New Works Programme when a pair of high speed lifts was installed in one of the disused Central Line lift shafts in an attempt to speed up the time it took to clear the platforms, but the station remained a major bottleneck only relieved by total reconstruction. The Victoria Line works involved the provision of a huge new ticket hall beneath the 'Circus' and many new escalators. The existing pair of Central Line escalators (and the old ticket hall) were retained but only for outgoing traffic. The new arrangements were largely introduced on 29th September 1967, for the purposes of Central Line traffic, and proved to be a major improvement. Towards the end of the decade it became clear that the existing station facilities at Debden were no longer adequate and plans were drawn up for a new, enlarged station building and ticket hall. Work commenced in the early 1970s and was substantially completed in 1974.

A significant milestone was reached between 1964 and 1966 with the rundown of freight traffic in the various goods yards at the eastern end of the line, owing mainly to the desire of British Railways to concentrate goods traffic at fewer, but larger, depots. Goods traffic had been run mainly at night to avoid interfering with the frequent electric train service and had been hauled by steam locomotives, the trains reaching the Central Line freight yards via the former LNER junctions at Leyton and Newbury Park, although the connecting line between Seven Kings and Newbury Park was closed in 1957. Traffic was run down quickly and all the yards were closed and the tracks lifted. Except at Grange Hill (and Eagle Lane, which was between stations), the yards were all converted into car parks for Underground passengers. The link between Leyton and the Eastern Region junction remained for a few years more for the use of a few Eastern Region staff trains which ran between either Liverpool Street (ER) or Stratford and Epping until 1970; the junction was later lifted and Leyton signal cabin closed.

The 1960s saw two major Acts of Parliament which influenced the political control of London Transport. The Transport Act 1962 caused the demise of the British Transport Commission and the setting up from 1st January 1963 of the London Transport Board as a nationalized industry. The Transport (London) Act 1969 then placed London Transport under the policy control of the Greater London Council through the medium of the London Transport Executive from 1st January 1970. A significant portion of the eastern extensions ran beyond the Council's boundary, which in later years caused different policies to be adopted with regard to fares and service levels along the Essex portion as compared with those in the GLC area.

Throughout the Central Line escalators had superseded lifts at many stations during major reconstruction work and many of these machines were beginning to get old. Some had already been replaced, but in 1976 a scheme of modernization was started to update many of these machines. Lifts still existed at Holland Park, Queensway and Lancaster Gate, and during the late 1970s and early 1980s these were replaced by more modern lift equipment. During the same period station lighting was also updated with a programme of fluorescent tube lighting replacing incandescent bulbs at those stations which still had them.

The post-war capital expenditure restrictions had resulted in many stations becoming dowdy and partially unkempt, and these were becoming sufficiently unattractive to adversely affect traffic levels. Since it had been perceived that passengers placed a rather greater weight on an attractive environment than had hitherto been thought, a major scheme of station modernization was begun. Fortunately the capital was available to do this in the lull between buying new trains, which are very expensive. Under this scheme major stations were extensively modernized and on the Central Line this work has been undertaken at Shepherds Bush, Marble Arch, Bond Street, Oxford Circus, Tottenham Court Road, Holborn, Chancery Lane, St Paul's, Bank and Liverpool Street (the latter in conjunction with the rebuilding of the main line station). At least some refurbishment has been undertaken at most of the other stations too.

Traffic levels on the Central Line have become very unequal, with severe overcrowding on the section east of Liverpool Street not balanced by the traffic offering on the Ruislip branch, which has not developed as hoped and where the train service has had to be thinned out over the years – something of an irritation with so large a depot as Ruislip at the end of the branch (some of the space has been put to better use as a track fabrication depot). Neither is the line east of Debden heavily patronized, and beyond Epping the long journey time to central London has not proved attractive in view of competing facilities and some level of economy has been necessary on the Epping–Ongar shuttle service, especially out of the peaks. From October 1976 the passing loop at North Weald was taken out of use so that only one train could be operated, on a 40-minute headway. More than one attempt has been made to close the line on the basis of the enormous operating costs as compared with the revenue earned. This has been refused by the Minister responsible but after the last occasion the line was reduced in December 1982 to run in peak hours only, and Blake Hall station – in its agricultural setting – was closed. A replacement bus service was inaugurated between Epping and Ongar, calling at

Tottenham Court Road platform after modernization in the 1980s. Nearly all the platforms on the original section of railway have now been completely updated.
London Underground Limited

North Weald.

A significant development affecting the administration of the Central Line occurred on 29th June 1984 when the London Transport Executive passed from Greater London Council control to that of the Secretary of State for Transport and was re-styled London Regional Transport. Under a provision of the London Regional Transport Act a subsidiary company was established on 29th March 1985 called London Underground Limited, and on 1st April 1985 London Regional Transport's railway activities passed to this subsidiary company.

The proliferation of extensions opened after the war created the need to identify the destinations of the trains by means of platform equipment, and signs were erected which in the central area identified the first two trains. During the mid 1980s a programme was initiated to install modern electronic train describers on the Central Line, where information was imparted by a 'dot matrix' display. These describers can also show how long it will be before the trains arrive as well as having the capability of showing other messages.

When the Central London Railway opened (as also the ex-LNER components) the ticket offices were built such that the ticket windows were along one wall of the booking hall. During the 1920s it became the practice to install free-standing ticket offices, known as Passimeters. However, by the early 1980s many of these old offices no longer matched modern standards for working conditions or security, and as part of a new systemwide ticket issuing system new or reconstructed offices are being provided at every station. The new offices are all of the 'wall' type and many involve additional major reconstruction or re-arrangement of the booking hall areas.

The Central Line is in the fortunate position of requiring rolling stock replacement at about the same time as the signalling has become life expired and this allows the possibility of undertaking a major scheme of modernization to take advantage of the need to update both simultaneously. Three prototype 4-car trains have already been delivered and are of a new type which incorporate many novel features. These will be evaluated and tested in passenger service, though not on the Central Line, before the bulk orders are placed. The new signalling will be controlled by computers and supervised from a central control room at Baker Street, all existing signal cabins being closed down. With new trains, new signalling, modernized stations and the new ticket system, there is no doubt that the Central Line will, for a while, become the most modern on the whole system.

A view of the future. Three prototype trains were delivered in 1987 for testing prior to ordering new trains for the Central Line. Each train is slightly different and the production trains will incorporate features resulting from the tests with the prototypes.
London Underground Limited